*the Bob and Weave*

# the Bob and Weave

poems

## JIM PETERSON

🐓 RED HEN PRESS | *Los Angeles, California*

*the Bob and Weave*

Cover art: *Bobalicon* by Francisco Jose de Goya Y Lucientes
Courtesy of the Cecil Higgins Art Gallery

Book and cover design by Mark E. Cull

ISBN: 1-888996-65-X
Library of Congress Catalog Card Number: 2005932470

Published by Red Hen Press

The City of Los Angeles Cultural Affairs Department, California Arts Council, Los Angeles County Arts Commission and National Endowment for the Arts partially support Red Hen Press.

First Edition

## Acknowledgments

*Amicus Journal:* "No Trespassing"; *Carvings on a Prayer Tree* (a chapbook, Holocene Press, 1994): "Guises"; *Cincinnati Poetry Review:* "The Return"; *Clockwatch Review:* "Turtles"; *Connecticut Review:* "The Large World"; *Cutbank:* "Linda and the Cowboy"; *The Devil's Millhopper:* "The Word"; *EMRYS Journal:* "Hammock," "Letting the Dog Lie," "The Man Who Heard"; *Figs & Thistles:* "Freedom" (as "Balance"); *Great River Review:* "No Bite"; *Greensboro Review:* "Cup"; *45/96* (an anthology of South Carolina poets, Ninety-Six Press, 1994): "Guises"; *In A Fine Frenzy: Poets Respond to Shakespeare* (University of Iowa Press): "As If"; *Interim:* "Rope of Needles"; *Kansas Quarterly:* "Blackhawk"; *King Log:* "Bear," "Inside," "Days"; *Mickle Street Review:* "Whitman: A Wrestler of Trees"; *Negative Capability:* "Ties"; *Nexus:* "Sweetness"; *Poem:* "The Dock," "Emptiness," "Black Skimmer"; *Poetry Comes Up Where It Can* (The University of Utah Press, spring 2000, the *Amicus Journal* decade anthology): "No Trespassing"; *Portfolio:* "Night Horses"; *Sun Dog:* "Moving On"; *Whetstone:* "The Power"; *The Wofford Journal:* "Food"

# Contents

## The Necessity of Evil

*Epilogue*

*As always*

*For Harriet, Jewelle, Gayle, and Patti*

*And in memory of my father, James*

The first part of the movement is the "bob." If you imagine your head as a cork floating on water and the opponent's fist as the surface of the water, when the hook comes at you, bend from the waist straight down to just below the water's surface (the fist). Remember to keep your head up enough so you see the eyes of your opponent.

The "weave" is a movement in which, after you "bob" you move your head sideways and up above the water's "surface" to your opponent's "dead side." That is to the side from which the hook came. This leaves you close to your opponent where you can still counter effectively. "The dead side" and "the live side" of your opponent is understood if you imagine your opponent as having the live side (where his hands are) and the dead side (towards the opponent's back). The live side is where he can hit you and the dead side is where you are safe. So, the "bob and weave" is a movement best used against a hook but which can be used against a straight punch. You move down under the punch then to the side and upward behind the punch to the "dead side."

—Ken Winokur

*Prologue*

## The Days

no one told me it would be like this
every day the sky grows dark
every night the sky grows light
the room holds its breath
and I enter
the walls continue to join each other
settling into corners with little cracking noises
under the paint

no one told me
that where there is a room
even a room still learning how to breathe
people will come
they will stand around with drinks in hand
if drinks can be had
or sit in rows and listen
I join them and I drink
and I try to remember the words

# Fields of Red Clay

"Heroes—like rules—are made."
—A friend, standing mid-lake and precariously in his aluminum canoe.

# As If

*". . . the dream in which I was Shakespeare . . ." A friend.*

When I was Shakespeare,
the weight of a new manuscript under my arm
bound and tied with leather
was enough to sustain the fight in me.
And my hands, which wanted nothing more
than to turn the pockets of strangers inside out,
curled up like fists even when I slept.

When I was Shakespeare, the moon
etched my face on the windowpane,
the sun carved my shadow in the dust
and the dogs abandoned by the dead
could not obliterate it.

The critics who sat in the galleries,
who never felt the rain on their heads
in the midst of soliloquy,
who never tasted the cold roots of originality
bitter and foreboding in their mouths,
scribbled their tiny paragraphs, their palsied puns,
then avoided my eyes later in the pub
as if I ever gave a good god damn.

## Food

It was growing dark
at the Capitol Café.
Outside, cars passed
through our straight
faces in the window's
glass. Our eyes met
and you glanced away.
An old man in the street
looked up, and his
face merged with mine,

smoker's squint, week-old
beard. He took a step
and for a moment his face
was in yours, your blond hair
to the shoulders, your
slim upper body, his face
twisted by some vision
beyond the help of sex
or prayer. Our food
came, and I remembered

the time we stopped
for a man who'd fallen
drunk in front of our car.
We helped him up, drove
him to a house he said
was home, left him sitting
on the curb. I think you
remembered too, but this
night we stared at our
food until it was gone,

heads bowed and mouths
chewing, nothing new to say
to each other. We split the check
and paid. Outside, the man
had found a shadow and slid
down against the wall.
Now that we could hear
his voice, we could not
make sense of the words.
But I was sure it was

a woman he spoke to,
the impatient, disbelieving
tone, rage without teeth.
Was he deranged, or only
drunk? This night we had
no car. A cop would
give him only more grief.
Should we stand him up,
escort him to the nearest
cab? He took a swing

at you, kicked out at me.
You slipped a ten into
his pocket. We stepped away,
turned our backs, kept
on walking, until the growl
of his voice sank into the sound
of passing cars. Your hand
curled around mine
and held it tight.

## Blackhawk

### 1

On a curve in the Rock River
Blackhawk stands straight on the slant
of the hillside, still as the trees
around him, forearms locked across his chest
that rises to the long line of his shoulders.
The vulnerable neck
presents the Hawk's head,
the sharp, distant eyes alive in a deep shimmer
of trees and animals and wind and water
that flow in his valley beneath and beyond him.

Though he is not an old man
the rings of age press out from him
with the power . . . .
And his people, feeling the animal in themselves,
dance in a circle around the fire,
drum giving its beat to their hearts,
and they make sounds like the animals—
the squawk, the roar, the hiss—
and give themselves names after animals
for they live with the terrible noise
of the perfect joy and suffering
of animals.

When the Sauks and Foxes fled across the Mississippi,
the face of Illinois paled with the fall
of trees and animals
and the growing expanse of the white man's farm.
But Blackhawk rallied his Sauks,
refused to give up his land,
allied himself with Pottawotamies, Kickapoos.
In his black boots and awkward stride
Lincoln marched down the valley with a band of men
and massacred the Sauks, Pottawotamies, Kickapoos,
preserving President Jackson's ever changing
permanent Indian Frontier.

Soldiers finally captured Blackhawk
and his son Whirling Thunder,
bound them and shipped them East
where they lived in a cage like animals
in a traveling circus till they died.
White men dug up Blackhawk's grave

and stole the body.  The Governor of Iowa
bought him and hung the broad skeleton in his office,
then later in a museum,
a popular curiosity for years.

2

On a curve of the Rock River
Blackhawk stands straight as the trees
in a stone blanket tower to the forearms
that lock across the widening chest
rising to the long line of his shoulder
that breaks where the vulnerable neck
presents the Hawk's head, the sharpened eyes.

The stone tower darkens in the heat of the sun
as if feeling for the first time its own weight,
becoming black as a kind of flesh
that bends to the animal shape,
its stone blanket splitting into wings
angling above the trees
in a trembling black V
that snaps down, breaking limbs.

He drifts up into the bright noon sky,
the burning circle of the sun
sharpened by the shadow of the Hawk
where it cuts black and deep
across the land.

A broken stem drops from a tree
into the spider's web,
but she doesn't spring, content
that her prey cannot escape.
A rabbit hunkers in the barbed brush,
breathless and still beneath the owl
who wakens in the sudden darkness of a shadow.
Bluejays and sparrows quit their quarrels.

Blackhawk's wings collapse against his flanks
and his body arcs into a dive,
elongates between the hook beak
and the black tail feathers,

a black arrow in the brightness of the sun.

While on the land
the black spot of his shadow
widens in a circle from out of the trees
across fertilized fields,
across hogs and cattle fattened to be killed,
the long-maned pony tied to a fence post,
show horses secure in their stalls,
the white frill of curtains in the farmhouse window,
the pragmatic square of the hay-filled barn,
the steel-glazed four lane highways,
the flat geometry of suburbs

into the bright stone steel and glass spires
of Milwaukee and Chicago
shuddering in the earth's rising heat.
The shadow stalls each city,
creeps through the white man's busy gaze
into the soft brain rippled with intelligence,
feels what no surgeon's blade
would ever reveal, recedes,
and the white man moves on
among the cars and trucks,
the battered arch of buildings.

Blackhawk still stands on the bank of the Rock River.
Holiday crowds shuffle around the statue's base.
The fire of the hunter's eye sleeps in cold stone

above the flash of trout and the storm
of cottonwoods in a morning wind.
The bluejay dips below the swooping sparrow,
the owl falls back to sleep
listening to the skitter of mice.
The spider returns in disappointment from the stem.

A hawk circles overhead,
its shriek not anything like words—
not meaning anything like hate, or revenge.

## The Peasant I Should Be

560 years ago I am the peasant I should be.
I pack the old horse with my vegetables
and lead him to the village market.
The silhouette of a tree in the wind
is a woman's face and hair,
the intermittent light of her eyes,
and suddenly she is everywhere:
she is the red fox trotting ahead of me on the path
to distract me from her brood.

She gathers the swallows from out of the hedges
and bids them to body forth into air,
bids all of the hands and hearts to rise up
from the battlefields at Compiègne
like all of the leaves rising up in another wind.

The skull of Joan of Arc on the Dauphin's table
still cradles the voices of Catherine and Michael and Margaret,
the flame of her body like a child's dress on the line
of a breezy summer day. Or like a prayer
catching all that's left of breath
in the ash of ten thousand bones.

## Nowhere

When there is nothing left to amuse us,
doors will remain open to the street,
the sun will cut into our rooms,
we will sit in the shadows
humming to ourselves
the partial memories of songs—
anything will do,
even the tick of an old watch.

When a child tells of the face he saw
in the window of a passing car—
an old face with unmoving eyes,
a black car shaped like the wind in a painting—
there will be laughter and speculation,
his father will kneel to him eyes to eyes
and praise him for his magnificent speech,
his mother will lift him with a groan
and call him *love*.

When the old man riding in the back seat
turns in the silence of fine leather and tinted windows
to the empty space beside him,
smoking the last good cigar,
he will ask his dead wife *Who is it*
*that empties the streets*
*of people and light?*
*What is it that makes*
*faces too thin for their eyes?*

When a traveller comes home,
lets the pack slide down from his shoulders,
and finds the nearest shade of a wall,
he will tell of the deaths of roads—
the return of nowhere—
a place without hedges and gates,
beyond the reach of satellites and repeaters,
thick with the new growth of neglect.

# Ties

You strolled whistling
through the front door, pulled
your loosened tie from your throat
and hung it on a chair.
The growing darkness of the afternoon
was light enough
for us to play among the big spruce trees.
Footballs and baseballs and whiffle balls
rained down in the air of those years.

Then came the day
when you left the tie loose around your neck.
You hustled us and dinner to the table
while the sun was still whole
above the roofs and power lines.
Then you snapped that tie back up to attention
for some game not including me
beyond the trees.

On that day I learned to hate
your disappearing car, your happiness.
No longer did darkness hang in upper limbs
for us to finish our unimportant games.
No longer was the air filled
with catchable throws, with the laughter
of a wrestling match you let me win.

More than once in my dreams
I grabbed the leering tie around your neck
to lead you like some docile beast
back into the yard
only to find an effigy of you on wheels
when I turned around.

One day I just stopped caring.
I started finding my own new games,
no guarantee of laughter or anything else,
sometimes in darkness or in crowds,
beyond the diminishing trees.

# Meat Cove

We saw him in all the lines:
grocery, postal, license, theater—
friendly elbows and round-toed sneakers.
He slid into his front row seat just in time

for the darkness to gather round,
and then the spectacle of images
flashed on his angular face—
his laughter, his silent tears.

We greeted him in the lobby,
exchanging judgments on the story.
Solitude and joy were the themes he saw.
Until, one gray day — the sun

a smudge of light filtering through clouds —
he began to sing in the town square.
Not an opera we wanted to hear
under the afternoon oaks and maples

that surrounded city hall with shade.
But he would not waver from his words
of wind in a lost forest and monumental stones.
Little girls danced around and mocked him.

Boys threw beer cans at his head
but he only flinched and kept singing
of the sheer cliffs of Meat Cove where natives
drove the caribou to their deaths.

His arms reached out in melodramatic embrace.
Someone called the cops, but this was not
a matter that would make them hurry.
We had to listen to his warbling migrations

of juncoes, his cracked confluence of rivers.
Two cruisers pulled up, sirens scattering
the boys and girls like flies, blue lights
crawling over the square like escaped faces.

Four cops cuffed him and read his rights, bent
his head down to fit into the black and white.
The day-shift maintenance engineer at city hall
had to pick up every last empty before dusk.

## The Bob and Weave

1
When I was small I would lie for hours
in the island-country of your bed,
dreamless and awake, your fingertips
smoothing the skin around my eyes and mouth.

Years later on August nights
I ran for you in parking lots,
slicing through asphalt circles of light
like some undiscovered particle of physics
while you counted laps in your Cadillac.
I lifted weights in the basement,
staining the big canvas mat with sweat.
In the fall I ran onto the chalk-lined field
to fight the boys from Aiken, Greenwood, or Augusta.
Sometimes I could see you leap to your feet
in the grandstand beside my mother.
I could hear your shouting.

Today I stand beside your bed
not quite believing that any moment
you won't rouse from this sleep
the doctors say is final,
sit up straight and look around to find me,
cough the tube from your throat,
and begin to speak.

2
You slept until nine, but the earthmovers
cranked up at dawn: pastures and woods flattened
into fields of red clay. You unrolled plats
on the hood of your car, holding the corners
down with shards of brick. You pointed and shouted
over the noise, and slowly, because you insisted,
walls rose up from the earth, houses spread over the hillsides—
malls, apartments, banks, restaurants.

At dinner you worried aloud
if I were man enough to make it
on my own out in the real world.
When you stood and straightened your tie
announcing you had business at the office,
Mother rushed to the mirror in her room
to brush her hair,
not wanting to hear the snap of the lock
as you pulled the door shut.

On your way out to the real world,
you smelled of good cologne,
your pockets full of keys
to empty houses.

3

Sometimes at night in the basement
you practiced the bob-and-weave,
showing me where to hold my fists,
how to shuffle on the balls of my feet
and to throw a straight left jab
like that loud-mouth Cassius Clay,
the KO punch building in my right shoulder and fist
like a terrible sneeze
reloading again and again.
But your hands were quick,
gloves rebuffing my roundhouse haymakers
like mud from a moving wheel,
your hands flicking—HA!—
like the twin heads of rattlers
between the curled noses of my gloves
to my reddening face.

4

It's August again,
and if I could run for you
I guess I would. I'd let you
count the laps until my mind was full
of nothing but my own breath
and the sound of your engine idling.
Outside this hospital window
no leaves blow over asphalt.
A hired man trims and edges the lawn.
Street lamps flutter on at dusk.
I have walked away
from your work and your money.
I have no son to carry your name.

The fields of red clay multiply
under every morning's moon.
In this room where you lie in a coma,
my fears and dreams coalesce
like the segments of a broken bone.
There is nothing you can build,
no new woman you can touch.
In your house I learned love
and suspicion, as if they were one.

But in this room
the pale wax paper of your skin gleams.
Even you have abandoned all the lessons
of your dreaded father
that you handed down to me.

For a few moments you awaken.
Nurses scramble to find a doctor.
The tube in your throat prevents speech,

your hands too weak to remove it.
In your eyes I can see you have come back
from one real world to another,
In this one, you have found your son again
but can speak to him only with your eyes.
For the first time since I was twenty
you know something I want to know.

## Mentor
### for JD

This giant, this man with a ten gallon hat,
stands before the elevator, guitar case swinging
from the great mollusk of his hand.
Is it only the dead who can dwarf a door
while the rest of us swirl around him
like leaves in a creek around a boulder?
Is it only the dead who can break from the ocean
of my memory and crash back down again
for a dive to the deepest floor?

The loose bones of his bracelet crawl
over the seminar table.  He announces
the rules:  This is the living
room of the believable outrageous lie.
This is the crater of cracked dreams.
This is the predatory grace of a word
dropping on its prey from a branch.  This is the poise
of a line that holds itself like the head of a snake.
This is the voice that fears not the guffaw
nor any cause of the guffaw.
                              He gathers the sentences
and dismembers them, scatters the fragments
across the page—the luminous bleached runes
of a dream, growing tooth by horn by tusk
into my dream.  I too must become ruthless
to break him, break him down into noise,
into skin, into single words deprived
of the relevance of their kin, into one eye
bereft of the resonance of its twin.

On this final day of class he speaks
of the master archer, the arrows of the student
that will return again and again to kill him, to spill
his wild-ass, vainglorious blood into the sand,
into the red clay, into the deep-clawed roots.

# Whitman: A Wrestler of Trees

Why would an old man undress
in the woods, summer gone,
autumn swinging in the trees,
a long year's second childhood
stinging the skin?

He lies naked in the grass,
crooked cane like a dead snake beside him,
gnats in a swarming mist around him,
his body moving in small ways
like an animal's to keep the flies off,
eyes fixed points against
the lazy motion of breeze and grass.

He puts his cane to work and stands,
slumped like a wounded bear
making himself a target
for the second time, one leg
little more than dragging,
a stillness deciding
to move, having drawn into itself
all that eyes and time in a single place
can draw.

Nestled into sapling thicket
on the side of a hill,
an old easy chair overlooks a small pond,
the stuffing, like dandelion seeds,
wandering on currents of air.

The old man sits, listens,
elbows pressed
into the chair's flabby arms,
backs of his knees hooked snugly
over the cushion's lip, naked feet
twisted down into the cool, black dirt,
chair slowly dematerializing beneath him,
wind-thrown leaves
catching flat against his foot
before somersaulting away.

Finally he grabs the slender bough
of a young tree standing near him,
grip returning grip, a contest
between young men who still have something
to prove, the muscles in his forearm
distending once again, the young tree
trembling down past its roots,
the old man grappling with something
in the earth beneath him
that binds him to this time and place
for one more day,

to this world
of what the eyes and ears can do,
of what the fingers feel and make,
of what the tongue
will surely taste and say.

He allows the tree to spring back
to its upright stance.
He looks around wildly,
laughs like someone waking from a dream,

sings of the city of his youth,
the forest of his old age.

That's why he comes to this place,
comes naked, comes clean,
comes with words whirling out of him
like seeds.

# Cup

He said "entrance," letting his eyes
trace the carved white letters.
He pulled the sign up and carried it

home unnoticed, red dirt on the stake
staining the thigh of his jeans. He
hung it on his wall like a painting.

All afternoon he lay in bed and studied
this word that conjured a gate, a grill
of metal bars pulled back from a path

leading over grass and sand to a body
of water capturing sunlight in a million
disappearing cups. In the shallows

a woman stood in a small boat
removing her clothes, folding each item
and placing it in a large black sack

until she stretched herself upward,
white as a flash of light on water.
He could not move, but only witness,

falling deeper into some grief, his own
secret body arched and naked, a thin
pale vessel dissolving in the wind.

## Home Run

When I was a kid, there was a big field behind my grandmother's house next door. A canopy of chinaberry trees hung over the corner of fenceline farthest from my house. In the summer when it was hot this was the shadiest, coolest place I knew, and the remotest too, without leaving family territory. I was completely alone there, and I could see into neighboring backyards from the cover of sparse underbrush. In the other direction I could look out on the wide and deep vista of the field. It would have been difficult for anyone to see me. I would sit there sometimes for hours and invent games, mostly this home run derby thing where I'd hit little wads of tin foil with a brand new unsharpened pencil. The little wads would fly all the way out into the sunlight sometimes, and that was a homerun. As the afternoon sun sank lower, the shadows would grow longer and it became harder and harder to hit homeruns. I knew all of the names of the great players—Babe Ruth, of course, and Mantle and Mays and Mel Ott and Harmon Killibrew and Ted Kluszewski and Lou Gehrig etcetera—from many different eras—Musial and Williams and DiMaggio, and Hank Aaron who was still playing—and they would all have their turns at bat. But the main thing was the flight of the little wad of foil— the esthetics of it I guess—the way it would take off when I hit it just right, this shiny speck rising up in the shade almost touching the canopy of leaves and then breaking out into the light and sailing and sailing and finally falling into the cut grass. The crowd roared in my throat, roared for Mantle or Ruth or somebody—but roared too for me, my own private crowd who had paid their hard-earned money and here they were on their feet cheering for me as I broke all the records. Then, if it was a good wad of foil, I'd save it for re-use in my pocket, and if the pencil had been a good bat, I would store it away in another pocket, and I'd walk up the fenceline back home and go in the back and let the screen door slam. Mother would say *where have you been* and I'd say *in the yard*. She'd ask *what were you doing*, and I'd say *nothing*. Then I'd go into my room to wait for supper, which was almost ready. I felt great—no other way to say this—just felt like I was worth something. My father would come home from work and keep his tie on at the table because he was going back out again. All evening I would keep remembering that cool corner and the way I could lean my back against the metal post, the way the chain links closed into a solid wall when I looked down the length of the fence and squinted just right. The way the ball flew when I hit it, the way it landed so lightly and so far away out in the grass and the sunlight.

## Sweetness

He cultivates the interior sound of a tone
which makes him late for everything that matters.
Every night he sits down to dinner as his wife
and children are starting their dessert.

He finishes alone by stovelight
and the sounds of his wife deliberately
waiting for him in the living room.
Every morning he sleeps thirty minutes

too long, his own tone edging out
each alarm as it arises. His eggs are cold
and the bacon gone. At work he recognizes
others more and more by the backs

of their heads. Their eyes turn to him
and fill with surprise as if to say
what are you doing here now? I needed
you an hour ago. He eats alone, always

has enough, just barely, to pay for lunch,
thus never tips, unable to look his waitress
in the eye. He eats less and less and grows
thin as a runner. He feels affection for everyone

but begins to understand that the distress
produced in others by his chronic delay
is the energy that keeps him alive. There is
a space between him and the world and he

tunes it like one string of a violin.

One day, he holds the bow
to its note for one instant longer, and a sweetness
fills the space. His wife returns to bed
and there is time, her breath like the dampness

of flowers after rain. Breakfast is hot and the children
hug him on their way out the door. At work
the others grow patient and begin to take their cues
from him. At lunch time there is money

in his pockets, but he strolls past the diners
in windows and listens to that one note
like a thread running through the loop
of each breath. At night, in that space between

waking and sleeping, he holds the one note
on the one string and feels its vibration moving
into his hands and throughout the length
of his body. He knows, at last, he is dying.

## Your Friend

Your friend has finally found his hat,
spins it on his finger and laughs.
His teeth glow yellow when he grins.
He wants his toothpick, and he wants it

now. Smears the window
with his index finger. Licks his palm.
Your friend has been asking for you,
says you know all the secret switches

and the hidden paths of mystical
bugs. Your friend has spoken his vows
to the chair and won't move, says
only death will part him. He has eaten

the real roses right out of the vases.
Swallowed the lucky penny he found
under the jam basket. You must come
right now and pay your friend's tab.

He has taken off his shoes and hung
his socks on the back of the chair.
Scratches his toes with a plastic straw.
He sings show tunes of the thirties

and our customers are leaving, the ones
who eat efficiently and tip with a smile.
Your friend is on the floor now,
has pulled the tablecloth around him.

He implores our new waitress,
the high school girl with pigtails,
to take off her clothes and dance.
Pretends he has a gun under there.

Wiggles his toes. Asks for a condom
and a bottle of rum. Says to stay calm
because you're on your way. He says
you always know what to do.

# The Man Who Heard
### for Arpad Darazs

They wanted to say something.
They could feel it
while sweeping the porch, driving to work
or watching
the red-tailed hawk circle overhead.
In grocery stores and libraries
their eyes met in brief, unexpected
harmonies.  Sometimes
sounds erupted from their throats
like the outbursts of children
on a playground.  Sometimes
the sound behaved,
coaxed to the shower, crooning.

Then a man arrived who held
this urge in the palms of his hands.
In streets and buildings
the voices found him,
curling up at his feet.
He led them to an empty room.
There was no question,
something in them wanted
out, and they obeyed.

When he raised his hands
the voices awoke as from a dream,
poised on the edge
of a sound definite and clear
he'd heard all along.
He moved his hands
and all those voices, separate and together,
called to the hollow places
in people for miles around.

When the singing stopped,
the message was a thousand faces,
silent for an instant in the dimness of the hall
before their own prolonged outburst:
We are here.  We are one.

## The Convex Face

"Well, the Zennists and other Buddhist types speak of emptiness. But
clearly there is emptiness, and then again there is emptiness."
—A friend, after pouring five fingers of single malt scotch into a tall glass.

## Grounded

He lies at the creek's edge, amazed.
Old voices dip and tumble over the stones.
They speak of soil and roots,
of swimming in the hole,
trout sparking in a spot of sun.
He takes off his shoes
and lets his feet down into the cold
where a child's cry curls between his toes.
How the currents reveal themselves.
The breezes leave no bird unturned.
The long shadow slowly fills the trees.
His feet break off and tumble downstream.
Much later he hears through the vines
that seagulls have made good use of them.
Maybe he will never move again.
Overhead the nighthawks are gasping.
His fingers get a good grip on the ground.

## Alone

To escape the three-lead electric-
guitar band and the blur of bodies
dancing under bad lights,

I staggered through the door
propped open with a sawhorse
into the night air that dried

the sweat on my face.  Between
parked cars, two men poured
whiskey into themselves,

laughter gurgling up through
the neck and into the glass bubble
above their heads.  I turned

the corner on humming neon
and slumped against the dark wall,
cinder-block cool against my back,

the grinning grills of a line
of cars still ticking like dying
clocks.  An arm's length away

fragments of a woman caught
the light of passing cars,
shoulder-length hair a black cape

around her face.  She sighed
a stream of smoke into the air
and extended her hand with a pack

of cigarettes as sudden and bright
before me as the head of a snake.
"Thanks, but I don't smoke," I said.

I wanted to reach across that space
and touch her hair or say something
to make her laugh knowingly and nod.

Instead, I leaned back against the blocks,
let my eyes rest on the one star
strong enough to show above the dark

heads of maples across the street.
We sat beside each other for half
an hour before she stood and dusted

off her jeans, her tired face
flashing neon red as she rounded
the corner.  I wanted to say,

"I'll take that cigarette now,"
wanted to draw that first smoke
into my lungs.  I ran back into

the heat and noise, but never could
be sure which one she was.  I stayed
until they closed, drank one beer

after another, and watched every
woman walk through that door
with a man, or with her friends,

or alone.  Later, far away from
that place, the air was cool, the sky
clear, and all the stars visible.

## The Guises

We left the sun behind us
as the trees threw out their shadows
and began to draw them back,
seeking in our separate ways
those same blue peaks on the horizon
growing sharper and darker
in the diminishing haze,
aware only dimly of each other
but already reaching for the guises—

those old mountains
like voices out of a cavern with bottomless pools.
Each of us grew small beneath them,
the white glinting of stone
under the spruce and fir,
clouds of mist drifting from hidden falls.

Everything had to be ferreted out,
even the spur of an ancient trail
in the silver glare of sunlight
among the she-balsams.
I was grateful for the shade of the first ascent,
chunks of smokey quartz
half submerged in the clay,
the trail unfolding before me
in rising switchbacks, exposed ridges,
descents into boulder fields
bathed again and again
in the scattering shrieks of hawks.

But neither of us could hear anything that night
above the din of stars,
waiting beside our separate fires
for the small target-faces of raccoons
drunk on the smell of coffee and bread.
All around us the birds
which give everything thoughtlessly every day
had entered their perfect sleep
while we lingered in our half dreams,
the night sky expanding to hold us both
turning in our voicelessness
like the small white ash floating above a flame.

# The Dock

I am able to find the dock
only at night, the dark sheet of the wind
caught against me, the cries
of invisible gulls drifting in
from that continent of water.

It isn't hard to stand at the edge
without fear, knowing that the piles
are strong and deep, that the rotting planks
have all been carefully replaced.
But what are those dark shapes that lie

far out on the surface under the moon?
Who is it that sometimes waits
like a tree hulking in the wind,
barring my exit until dawn?
The small boats return

as empty as the answers I have tried.
Do the answers lie far out and at the bottom?
Or do they slide along the surface like eels?
The fishermen may know, their eyes
sealed open like fish, calling out

to me to help them secure, their voices
sudden blasts of memory in the long
silence of water, their hands still red
with working in the salty cold.
I give them a lift up with hands

still warm from pockets, and join them
as they waken to the land and sunlight.
But they talk among themselves,
voices too hoarse from the long night
for me to understand.

## The Black Skimmer

Daylight withdraws from the body
of water slowly like pain.  Dolphins

crest off shore.  Children point.
Far out a black skimmer on the wing

barks.  The tip of its long, lower mandible
cuts water, takes the sudden weight

of a fish, carries it (still alive, still
a silver flash) over the last glimmer

of the surface, past where waves
break, and drops on a shore rough

with broken shells.  Its white breast
and belly swell above the small eye

that cannot close.  Another skimmer
wheels and glides, red-footed,

crow sized, dropping down by levels
to my level, the calm look of its black

eye so well adapted to the sun-sprung
angles of water.  It veers to give me

space, and I turn to follow that flight,
the black flash of wings, the white

gleam of underparts, the red, black-tipped
blade of a beak dipping down for more.

## Night Horses

A wind blows down from the hill
where the horses stand,
eyes so full of watching
their bodies have become smooth marble.

These yearlings and two year olds
have never been coerced by men,
running loose in overgrown pastures
on an old farm abandoned by everything
but the county records and the kudzu.

Stunted from erratic grass and worms,
in the daylight they are ferocious cowards
galloping, whirling, blowing hard, raising up
into giants with unfeeling fists.

At night they stroll
in the soft wind oozing from the forest.
I sit on the side of the hill
and they gather round—
great somnambulists.

The soft skin of an upper lip touches my cheek,
nibbles at my hair and shirt
like a young man dallying with his lover's blouse.

Pine trees groan in the wind.
The tin roof on the old barn bangs.
Quiet snorting, the casual tearing of grass,
deep molars sliding, crunching.
The horses' big black eyes repeat
the bright circle of the moon.

## The Hammock

At dawn when the old one wakes
speaking his own name, William ... William,
he feels the stiffness stretching
down his back like a cold wire
and thinks of the children.
Remembers how close death comes
in the dream, a small hand reaching
for his to lead him
into some slow game
where the lights are gradually dimming,
the moves no longer clear.
Later, he will eat
because the children are there,
gobbling fast toward their games on the lawn.

It's not that he loves children
any more than he hates death.
It's just that their eyes still hold
a piece of the darkness
that comes before life. Their voices,
a touch of the emptiness
of not wanting.
Sometimes at night
his great granddaughter crawls into his lap,
both sleeping for a while
in the hammock of their dreams,
swinging in the silence between two trees.

## The Return

when you cannot find the page
to pick up where you left off
when the match refuses to strike
when two people who have known each other too long
turn for the first time from their dreams of each other
to each other

it returns

it often moves at dawn
sliding beneath the doors
like leaves
unaware of the strength of its own limbs
the incredible lock of its jaws
the chill of its own breath
hanging always like the body of air
in the eye of a tunnel

there was nothing it did not consume
and nothing it did not replace
though Mary and Paul were not so sure
trying to put all their fingers on it at once
noting that in the midst of differences
all was the same

it is here even now though receding
its long tail growing thinner
the eye in its tip looking up from the grass
for the strange smile
of someone completely alone

when the voices stop coming to terms
when the wood won't burn
and the cold leans flat against your back
with the face of midnight dark against the window
when you cannot go on any longer
when all is finally lost

it returns

# The Word

The night sings in my window,
chuck will's widows
overlapping like echoes,
cicadas sliding up the scale
to find a note they hold for ages.
My dogs dig in the sand
and lie down again.
My neighbor slams his door
and drives away,
twenty miles to the city,
slowing down only for red lights
in vacant streets,
asphalt shining like the surface of water.
He parks beside a building
where the lights are never out,
stacks bundles of paper
in the back of a truck,
then floors it into years of concrete,
throwing a million words
into empty corners of the night,
stepping again and again
into the clutch as deep as his leg,
loving the gearshift's grind against his palm
and the long stretches of speed,
leaning into corners at thirty, then forty,
saluting other drivers breaking past
as they deliver us from our special needs,
themselves delivered from the silence
by country music on the radio
where all the good and bad things occur
like in the news.
Whatever happened to the word?
The cicadas sing as if they know.

## The Power

1
The wind cannot penetrate
the long hall of horses.
I feel nothing but the weight
of their silent response to me.
I see nothing but the scars
of leftover moonlight.
I hear nothing but the soft plunk
of my feet in the stray oats and straw.
I find the switch on the wall
and down both sides of the barn
their long sleepy faces emerge.
I lead the big stallion outside,
tack him up quickly by starlight,
slide him into a slow canter
over the dirt road and through the pines.
The cup of an ear pricks back to listen.
My mind falls down, falls down into haunches,
my legs the subtle-shifting
root nerves of both our bodies.
I can feel in my body
the weight of each hoof thrusting
and falling, collecting the four
to the three beats of the canter,
my butt smooth-falling
at the calm center of the saddle,
pushing his body against the steady
contact of my hands on the steel bit
that splits the back of his mouth.
The limbs cut in above and beside me.
I ride with my face to the mane,
his head and neck lunging down
as he gathers himself to launch us
through a long climbing tunnel of trees
till we spring into the field of light

and into the flow of young slash pines
that slant to the west in a low groundswell
of darkness around and beneath me.
I hear you galloping
your long-legged mare
on the trail behind me,
til you've joined me.
We reach out as before,
our hands entangled
in the air between us
as all things grow together
in the speeding darkness around us,
the power flowing from beneath us,
churning the earth back behind us.
I cannot see you clearly,
your face a mask of moonlight and leaves,
cannot feel you apart from the knot
of our hands suspended between us.
These animals know where they're going.
No voice could shatter this stillness.
A stand of trees rises before us
and a broad path cuts through them
like a private peeling back of the waters
that bears us into swirling constellations
Of fireflies overwhelming the air.

2

For the sake of our horses we must rest.
I follow the fork to the pond and dismount.
His ears flop like a old mule's in the wind,
twin plumes of mist exploding in the air.
I can hear my blood still charging
from heart into brain and back again.
I can hear the wind sidling up to branches
and the close stamping of hooves,
the sucking of moonstruck water
into the great living barrels of bodies.
Wind-ripples flash on the surface.
The sandy trail glows like an arm
of the moon reaching down.
Hoofprints darken into craters.

I watch you standing beside me,
long reins looped down from your hand
to your horse's head buried in grass.
You turn to me, your face half in darkness,
half shining, your blond hair
mingling with bay mane, the circle
of your one visible eye, full of me.

## Incest

The birds said nothing all night long.
What was I expecting?
Some sort of news about the future of feathers?
Gossip about the goings on in some farmer's far field

where the jays and swallows are at it again?
I admit it. I expect a message
from something that isn't me
or even like me. No feathers,

no paper, no paragraphs parading
over one page after another.
The message started coming to me again
last October in the Tetons,

with the Grand One itself hovering
surrealistically in an icy gray sky,
and that other great hunkerer, Mt. Moran,
peeling the late light from its face:

a visceral quality of silence due maybe
to six inches of fresh snow laid down overnight
or maybe to the rawness of rock and pine.
Or to some hopeful state of mind

that has haunted me all of my life:
The birds are talking now but still
say nothing, and these words of mine
are equally nil. I lean in this doorway

and forget the done and the undone of inside
and outside. A crossbreeze unsettles the dust
that drifts before me in a ray of light,
each particle seeking its brother or sister.

## The Convex Face

When we turn our soup spoon over at dinner
and observe our convex faces
expanded to the verge of breaking,

we may thus remember at such odd times
that we are only one among many,
that we take up a small space
that someone else will occupy soon enough,
that we are fulfilling effortlessly
our ancient biological privileges.

At that moment we are free to walk outside
and lie down on the cold ground
as if finding it for the first time
and sleep with our heads propped on a root,
with our hands folded on our chests
inside our half unbuttoned shirt for warmth,
our mouths falling open and vulnerable

to the unknown night.

## Crazy Wisdom

I sit on a couch and read
a book on "crazy wisdom"
thinking to myself yes
how crazy wise I am.
A large mosquito,
a king among its kind,
lands on my knee,
no flying below the radar
for this one.
I resist an impulse
to smash it.
I lay my book aside,
lean forward.
Entangled in my gnarly hair
it burrows down.
I place my finger in its way
and it climbs aboard
the whorled skin.
"Eureka!" it shouts
with a tiny bold voice
and drives into me.
I blow it away
into loopy circles
around the room.
It bumps the window
where the trees outside
jump in a gust of wind,
bumps the cactus, the fiddle,
the lampshade cloaking
the light by which I read.
Finally it dives onto my empty sock
screaming, "The scent! The scent!"
And there it remains
all afternoon,
sinking its long head deep
into that bloodless white cotton.

## Letting the Dog Lie

The horses thunder
in the fields tonight.
A breeze stays high in the pines.
The dog squeezes out
from under the house
and stares at the ball
till he falls asleep
curled around my foot.
For the first time in months
the air is cool.
The front door drifts on its hinges,
the old chair lounges on the lawn.
The horses rest,
lean over fences
pawing the ground,
inviting my hands to their faces,
to their withers and the sweet scratching spots.
The hammock sways
under loblolly pines
and Orion's belt,
but I'm stuck to the ground
by one foot
under the sleeping dog
who dreams of lightning and thunder,
of mud at the edge of the pond,
who dreams of the flight of old tennis balls
made better than food,
better than rolling in manure,
by the touch of these human hands.

## The Empty Bowl

A man's dog was very old and crippled. Each morning she only sniffed her food, giving it a few licks. Then she would drag herself over to an empty red bowl that had belonged to a previous dog. She would lick the empty bowl and shove it along the boards of the porch with her nose. The man would pick her up, crooning softly, "You must eat, Old Lady," and place her next to her own bowl of food. She would stand there and smack her lips a few times, then drag herself over to the empty bowl. The man tried different food, but that never worked. He tried putting the food in the red bowl, but she only reversed the process, sniffing the meaty morsels, then dragging herself resignedly to her own empty bowl. He tried removing one of the bowls, but then the old dog would haul herself around the porch, down the steps falling on her face at the bottom, then out into the yard and under every tree and bush looking for the empty bowl. So the man would put both bowls back on the porch to keep her happy. Every morning it was the same. The scruffy white hair of her muzzle, the raw floppy ears pestered by gnats and flies, that half-seeing gaze through cataracts. He couldn't understand how she survived without food. She looked so bad it embarrassed him for the neighbors to see her. "Maybe I should put her to sleep. That would be the merciful thing to do." All the way to the vet's office she lay on the front seat beside him with her head in his lap. If he took his hand away from her head, she would stare at him until he put it back. In the car there were no gnats or flies to nag her ears. No space demanding she drag herself here or there. When he arrived and lifted her from the seat, she was limp in his arms, pink tongue dangling lazily from her mouth.

*Witness*

The rumble of radials over the blacktop,
the cracked skull of the body found
among scrub oaks and slash pines,
blue shirt torn like sodden leaves.

The room with its seventeenth century
bureau and mirror,
overhead fan ticking its own brand of time,
bedspread pulled taut as fencewire from post to post,
chair piling up with worn but still fragrant
not-quite-ready-for-the-hamper shirts and blouses,
stack of books on the floor already read,
waiting for their slots in the shelf.

Shuffle of voices, movement of eyes:
in the midst of this dance remember yourself.
Keep turning and dipping and holding
the day with its long promises and dreams:
the mint breath of a colleague,
the giveaway halts of a client's complaint,
the willingness of a smile to take you home
and lick you clean for another night's sleep.

Remember yourself:
amazement at your own feet,
at the constant reassertions of your sex,
at the lightness of your hands
ready to unfold like bats and take to the night,
at the poised carriage of your head—
vulnerable, uncertain in its station over the heart—

and ask yourself
is there anything that remains after the flame
that is not ash?

## The Arc

an ant breaks
the boundaries of tribe
in the slick solitude
of a green blade

stained by rain and pollen
the concrete bench
is an old stump in a glade

I study this day
the crippling flavor
of earth and light

the wind rising to savor
the taste of a bird

the force of my footsole
on the root-bound path

the smell of an old rain
on the rocks

## Emptiness

The waters ease beneath my door.
The calls of the katydids are on the wind.
Tomorrow I will be no more.
Tomorrow the leaves will not follow
the whims of the breezes.
Tomorrow my throat will not open
with the vowels of old words,
nor will there be new words
forming in the foundations of my skin.
Tomorrow a darkness that has been called light
shall find my coiled thought
in the recesses of its lair.
Tomorrow you who have beheld my face
as I have beheld yours
will no longer touch my lips in greeting,
and the eyes which have known
the sweet sprawl of your limbs on the sheet
will disappear like raindrops into the earth.

# The Necessity of Evil

*"Archetype shmarchetype."*
—*A friend, upon waking from a near death experience following a severe blow to the head.*

## Inside

In the most fickle of Marches
a dog haunts my street.
No, it is a child.
My eyes are not so good.
She sings under the cottonwood.
She sits on my front porch,
a splash of gold and maroon,
an eyewatering blur of wind.
I watch her through my blinds,
her oblivion my wound.  What if I
trapped her in a glass jar,
kept her on a shelf in an abandoned room
where all the lights keep burning,
and I were outside, my skin
warming to the sun's promise,
my eyes alive inside my face.

## Join the Club

On this full-moon night
someone whispers your name
eerily into the thin gray space
beneath a door.  Someone raises
his cap on a stick outside the broken

windowpanes.  Is that really a crow
trapped in the room at the end of the hall?
The neighbor's dog half a mile away
will not stop barking.
You think of your hands buried in its fur,

its gray muzzle stroking your calf.
You make your bed in a corner
of a windowless inner room,
rake your small light
over the dream-stained walls,

over the hardwood floors that complain
under the weight of a single thought.
What will the others who've gone before
concoct under the shadowing moon?—
the girl who decided not to kiss you

in that last moment at her door,
the boy who hit you in the back
when the fight broke out.
Yes, you are grateful and afraid;
you will have years of nights

in which to sleep, years to call to order
the voices crackling like static in your head.
Your batteries have died, and courage
means to wait for whatever comes.  Is it friend
or foe creeping slowly toward you in the dark?

# Turtles

When I called to him from the shore,
he appeared from the mouth
of a distant cove,
glad for some excuse I suppose,

moments later gliding easily
into the narrow boathouse.
We sat on the grassy bank of his retreat
and tossed small pieces of bread

to the mallards,
laughing at the way they raced
to each tiny splash,
small bass and bream darting

like hungry shadows beneath them.
He loved how the winner lurched away,
stretching her neck
and holding her bill high to swallow,

until she screeched, her body
drawn backward and down, disappearing
in a bubbling whirlpool.
The others swam quickly away,

wakes merging behind them,
leaving the last crumbs to the fish.
"They're everywhere," he grumbled, rushing
into his house to get the gun.

## Linda and the Cowboy

Your old green cap is on the table.
The sun is finally breaking through.
Good old Cowboy Billy, solid as a phone pole
and half as tall, through the screen door
just a dark shape with a white grin
standing in the front yard, says the weather
is good for something and you'd better
come on out and collect what he owes you.
I tell him you're usually under that green cap
this time of day, but he doesn't laugh,
just grins, just grins, and says he'd hate
to hurt a woman on such a nice day
but I know he's all talk, and the wind
blows through and picks up your cap
and sets it on the chair. I figure you're
down at the creek for a swim or walked
into town for a beer and you sure
picked a fine time because old Bill's leaning
on the screen like a bear in heat
and grinning twice as big and says he's done
run you out of town, put you in the trunk
of an old Cadillac bound for Texas, and I say
sure, sure, and his hand hits the screen
big as a hat, a black hat, and I tell him
how hard we've worked to save this place
to keep it alive, and his hand breaks through
the screen and hangs in the air like some
fleshy thing in an old horror show
that sucks all the air out of my space
and I can't breathe and I've worked so hard
Just look at the blood in these walls
I tell him
just look at these hands just look at them.

*Freedom*

The day shifts its weight into the west.
The whistling of thieves from alleys,
important voices in restaurants hovering
over mixed drinks and cellular phones,
exhaust from the jammed streets
like a collective aura clinging to us,
our cars and buildings. A big yellow dog
lies under an old red Buick Skylark, panting.
In one doorway a tiny girl, her scuffed knees
turning blue, pink ribbons coming loose
in her long blond hair. In another,
three pigeons stand among cigarette butts.
For one hundred years, they have been watching.

A man slides down into the smudged folds
of his oversized raincoat, back
against the gray wall of the bar,
laceless boots tied once around
with string, neon beer signs
burning him red then blue.
He laughs to himself, long hair falling
like a dead claw over his face, hauls
himself up again and walks straight
to the end of the next block, the call
of another corner, the separating
sole of his right shoe drinking
the grainy air above concrete.

The lanes are clear. I could choose music,
but don't, my cubicle like Emerson's transparent
eyeball gliding under the changing lights.
The last bit of sun skims over the streets,
cats press their bellies to the ground
and grow still in the shadows. People
gather around their cars, still talking
of work. Somewhere, far out on the road
ahead of me, a doe lingers over a yellow
line, curiosity blazing in her eyes.
We claim that freedom is everything. My
son behind a chain-link fence is waiting,
listening for the *hum* of this small engine.

# The Business of Saturday

Water is the best transition from dreams.
Stand under the hot spray for ten minutes,
take your body into your own hands.

Chewing is the best passage from water.
I recommend raisins and granola—
your thoughts rising and falling
on the waves of passing cars.

Then, take care of business:
sort old postcards beginning with the Spanish geisha
who reaches with spell-casting fingers toward the dragon fish
and ending with the gray shades of Homer Spit
that stretches into Kachemak Bay,
Kenai Mountains rising beyond.

For half an hour
search bookcases for lapses in alphabetical order;
notice three books you intend to read
and lay them on the floor.

Then watch TV for three hours.
Avoid nature programs that feature hyenas,
their jubilant tearing of the young and weak.
Watch instead old sit-coms about talking horses;
let canned laughter be your guide.

And don't forget to study your desk:
cannon bone of a cow cracked and flaking,
two stems of sage no longer pungent,
reading glasses with scratched lenses,
the chaos of junk mail.

Now you can face the afternoon.

Wear a cap for the low line of the sun
and gloves to free your hands from pockets.
Don't be disturbed by the wildness of skateboarders
nor overly soothed by men watering their giant sunflowers.
The sidewalk is infinite though the day is dying,
but there is nothing to fear, nothing will be lost;
someone is canning those laughs twenty-four hours a day.
You will find your house soon enough in the dusk,
light leaking through blinds onto the brown grass.

## Autumnfest
*for Ruth and Ken*

On the appointed day three poets drove to the city
and stood on the festival grounds
before the still great house of a once great man.

Families gazed into portable stalls
where Confederate women churned butter,
where ceramic dragons reared and blew flames,
where pastel renderings of the low country
hung in gold frames.  In the field where the poets gawked,
ragtag Confederate soldiers ceremoniously
fired their rifles into ancient oaks,
the flanks of their good horses convulsing with each shot.
A cloud of gun smoke settled on the poets
under the weight of a slight rain.

The poets mused among themselves,
"Where are the officials who invited us to read?
Where are the podium and the microphone and the chairs?"
But no one could answer them,
so the poets began reading loudly to each other.
Behind them a big band recalled the thirties and forties.
Before them in the streets the bagpipes whined melodiously,
and on the vacant lot next door, rockers made love to their guitars.

For once the poets could not hear themselves think.
Huge drops of rain from an overhanging magnolia scored their pages.
They scraped their throats raw trying to make their words
heard, their music felt beyond the bones of their own bodies.
One man listened long enough to finish his corndog,
one woman long enough to rest her back,
then hefted her boy to her shoulders again
and went to look at the dragons.

Later the poets drove to an art bar,
huddling among the orange and blue heads,
and talked about fame,
how it had ruined the best of their kind.

## The Large World

The black cat turns his head, yellow eyes
calm, unblinking. Yesterday I chased
him off with rocks from the driveway,
trying to make my yard a haven
for my own cats. Now, my slender calico
slinks along the roof-line. My persian

hunkers in the top of a cottonwood.
And my oldest, the mottled gray we call
Mister, strong enough in the past
to defend the others, is frozen among
the blowing leaves. I think about the .32
my father left me, unfired in twenty years,

loaded, packed away in its black pouch
under the bed. But a shot would concern
the neighbors, and I know I am overreacting.
It is the black cat who is trapped — between
this hulking, bearded human and Mister
who is just desperate enough to be a threat.

When I was a boy stunned by stories
my older cousin told of the succubus —
a black cat the size of a woman who
could seep like smoke under the door
of a sleeping man and possess his soul —
I learned to fear all silent stalkers. Even

my own cats are banished from the bedroom.
Mister uncoils and the two are a tangle
of screams and fur among the shrubs.
The other breaks loose and vanishes
down the alley. Mister crawls out and limps
into the house. The wind gusts,

the leaves of the immense cottonwood
tear loose one by one. At night I still dream
of sleeping in the cold third-story room
of a vast house. Of waking with that
weight upon me, making my breath
her own. I want to look into the face

of my nightmare as that black cat looked
into mine. To yield my breath,
to inherit whatever world the breathless
know. Instead, I climb the ladder
to my roof, grab my whining calico
by the scruff, and bring her down.

## A Rope of Needles

1

he gave her stairs spiralling to perches in the Chinaberry trees
he gave her rocking chairs and a table and poured her a drink
made from the unpronounceable fruit of another land

with her own first words to him he wrote a beautiful song
but when he began to sing she withdrew into the mist
her last words fell like spoons on the boards


2

he found her strolling among hats and he bought them all
he bought her land under a bright sun that consumed the mist
each day was a different hat and he watched her dance
he built her walls and floors from the lava of an old volcano
he fashioned the windows out of which she leaned and waved
he made the limbs of trees twine in a circle around the house
made them stretch in a rich canopy for shade
from her own dreams he made a book of stories
but when he read she stepped back into shadows
he could not find her
he searched the book for clues
but her dreams were plotless tales
he followed her into the shadow but it was only darkness
he ran his hands over the cold bellies of his walls
but everywhere there was only the silence of hats

3
a year later he found her again in the forest
sleeping among roots and ant trails
he held her hands cold as the morning leaves
and pressed them to his face
he made her a cage he made her help made her carry
the steel bars made her gather the hats and burn them
together they worked getting rid of everything
even the mirrors that would not let go of their smiles
the chairs that stretched out under the moon

the bed in its dark circle where she would never sleep

the walls and roof which were havens for shadows
even the trees that held in balance the sun and the earth
together they stepped inside and pulled the iron door shut
he fell asleep with his hand on her hip and woke to the cold floor
to the sound of leaves underfoot in the darkness

he learned how to get along without food and water
he strained all his dreams through his fingers and made nothing
he loved the sun and its one spot of coolness at noon
the white light of the moon in the grass
the wind with its secret agenda and its constant interruptions
the rising tide of each breath

when she returned a year later she threw him a rope of needles
it ruined his hands but he could not release it
she built a fire in the night and the bars blistered his face
she opened the book of her dreams
where everything was known but nothing remembered

he could not tell her what to do

# Number One Fighter

He has learned to tolerate their hands. There is no training for the first fight, only waiting in a small room with one window too high to reach. Only a feminine voice from speakers telling Tom he has no choice, he will fight. He takes comfort from the fact that it is a woman's voice. The sunlight in his window for one hour each day is good, and Tom is grateful. And the food, though bland, is healthy, and he remains strong. He can see their faces, but he has learned to forget them instantly, to become ignorant of faces.

The fight takes place in a larger room. No windows this time, only a small camera dangling from each of the four corners. He has been given a dark blue costume, tight fitting. The other man's costume is the same, except it is white. Both men have a knife with a six inch blade. The door closes behind Tom, and he looks at the other man. Small but wiry. He will be quick. Tom knows he must get in an early damaging thrust, must use his superior strength. There are only two rules: (1) A fighter must not throw his knife. If he does and he kills the other, he will face the number one fighter next. (2) One fighter must die.

Early on, the smaller man proves his quickness. A skilled practitioner of the bob-and-weave, he slips Tom's every thrust and slash. Even his eyes are quick, shifting alertly in their assessment of Tom's feet and hands, never meeting Tom's eyes. And his hands are never still, like huge crazed flies whirling before Tom's face. Soon Tom has cuts on his forearm and both thighs. There is more blood on the mat than sweat. He is growing weak. Without thinking, he retreats a step, takes his knife by the blade and throws it. It is only in this moment Tom realizes his knife is a well crafted weapon, perfectly balanced. The way it releases from his fingers, the way it rotates in the air like the spokes of a wheel. The way it enters the small man's chest almost without a sound. How quickly the man with quick hands empties his life onto the floor.

For two days they are good to Tom. Good food, treatment for his cuts, time to rest. Time to contemplate the skills of the number one fighter. He requests and receives training in the bob-and-weave. Finally they strip him naked, give him his knife and shove him through another door. The mind has this power—to extend one instant into a great space. Tom finds the other man in a distant corner, also naked, a short, fat man with frightened eyes, a black splash of hair, already crouched with his left foot forward, right arm and hand extended before him and moving across his body which has already begun its forward curl into a tumble. Offense and defense packaged into one swift motion. The will to move explodes in Tom's chest—bob first, then weave. Already the air is full of spinning light.

## Real Estate

He punches in the lockbox code,
opens the door of someone's home.
His clients will be here soon,
their Saturday off, sweaters

with holes in the armpits
when they reach up to call attention
to their old friend: water damage.
He knows they are house-hunting

for sport, points acquired by catching him
in a lie: "That roof has got at least
ten more good years in it." The habit
of more than two decades selling

houses with Jaguars in the garage
and cut-glass dragons holding
the papers down on desks
with legs carved into ornate flames.

A young woman on TV convinces viewers
that God was born in Kansas
and is spreading the new good news
through The Modern Jesus Mid-American

Television Campaign. He turns it
off, makes a note to turn it back on
before he leaves. Just what he needs,
something else to think about.

Isn't it enough to have driven all the way
out here on his thirty-first consecutive
day of work without the whiff of a sale?
Isn't it enough he didn't bring his little girl

because all he wanted was the dead
quiet of his car with the windows rolled
up and the white line broken
into a thousand thousand entrances and exits?

Soon his clients will arrive in their Honda
that will turn two hundred thousand miles
any day, their yappy Pomeranian
scratching at the cracked window.

Pete and Sally touch the paintings
and furniture and fixtures only an interior
decorator could imagine, feeling up
the good life someone is ready to leave behind.

Then he waves good-bye to them, closes
the place up, remembers to switch the TV on
to Jesus.  Outside, the flash and rumble sky
promises rain that, once again, will not show.

# The Last Child

His first summer at the Home
he lured a stray bitch into the barn
and clubbed her to death with a bat.
He said she crumpled up
like a balled-up piece of paper on fire.
Said *that* would teach her
to spit her litters out
all over his land.
His second year at the Home he cornered
the director's daughter in the gym
and wouldn't let her pass.
I pulled him away and she ran.
He studied her routines,
was watching when she
walked home from school,
when she headed out on her bike,
when she rode on the front seat
of the white Cadillac
between her mother and father.
One night in his last few months,
he stole a neighbor's car,
drove it to the director's house,
tried to lure the daughter into the car
with a wrapped present,
but she kept backing toward the porch.
Ten minutes later he flipped the car over
on Highway 21 heading out of town.
Broken bones shut him up for a month.

Meanwhile I quit the Home—
too confused myself I guess
to be soother of savage children,
tired of being afraid all the time

of what he might do next—
and moved from job to job,
lived in mobile homes in one-light towns.
It took five years for the first time,
but he found me. The phone
rang: he'd changed his name
from Billy to Bill to Mister B.
He hit my door with the flank of his fist
and walked on in, looking around.
His pack was full of soiled underwear.
His red beard was longer than mine.
He needed a place to stay and money.
I found him a job with a friend,
but after three days Mister B knew
more about disk brakes than they did
and they booted him out.

The last time was the worst.
He wasn't interested in work.
While I was out he kept the blinds pulled,
drank beer, lit one cigarette off another
and watched porno on the tube.
When the neighborhood girls ganged up on him
with bamboo sticks,
I didn't even ask why,
just drove him into town,
put him up in the YMCA,
and gave him a hundred bucks.
Next day I quit my job and got out of there.
Even I didn't know where I was going.

It was okay when he talked
about his life on the road,

what it was like to sleep under the overpasses,
how the taste of discarded food was the best.
I enjoyed his descriptions of abandoned cars
where he would live for days,
of the women who were far enough
gone on drugs or booze to run with him
until he left them unconscious and alone
in the dry ditch of a park.
But I wanted to be a good neighbor to good neighbors,
I wanted to find a real friend.
I didn't care that he'd changed his name to Red,
that he considered himself the ultimate philosopher
of sleaze and degradation.
I hated that I listened, that sometimes I even laughed.

Two thousand miles and twenty years from the Home
and still he's found me.  He knows
I've seen him through the closed blinds.
I haven't had a date in years.
The last child I touched ran away
and cried in her mother's lap.
I part the blinds and study the way
he waits, the way wind blows trash
down that almost empty street.

## No Trespassing

I have walked here before,
entered a chain link gate
at the end of a narrow dirt road,
happy to see the weeds overtaking it
but knowing it is owned—
somewhere circled on a map.
I have arrived too late
to return home before dark.
I have gathered the seeds
in my cuffs and socks and laces,
undergone the inspections of owls and deer
as mindless in the moment of watching
as trees.
I have entered the mask of the web,
tiny builder diving for weeds,
have heard the voices come back slowly
to meet my silence
and have tracked the crackling of leaves
over the whole long face of a hill,

but never have I seen this place
in the light of so much moon and stars—
leaves and needles shining on the ground
and in the air.

I want to stand still forever.

# January Dusk in Montana

The moon is large, larger
than the heart on a child's sleeve
and so bright and sharp
in all its edges
it bursts—an immense silence—
its white hot shards tumbling
in the wind over the ridges and ranges
of Paradise Valley.
But wait, the snow still squeaks
beneath my boots.
Small leaves of sage, pale green,
break the surface.
I snap one stem
to retrieve its stalwart scent.
The headlights of a distant car
move slowly over the face of darkness.
The travelers do not hear
below the momentum of their voices
the emptiness beneath their wheels,
the earth opening wider and wider.

## Plenty

A trail laced with green needles
is silent on a summer afternoon,
not counting wind and flies,
as if the ridge were a giant bank

of time,
as if the clock stopped
in the last laser-light of a day
thickening with visible air.

A man like a stone
changing to earth stretches out
on the scored face of a field
and only breathes.

A thin early moon in the east
turns like a bowl,
and what is it pouring
into such stillness?

The man rises, becoming
more than breath again—
eyes and ears and dreams.  He takes
note of an old friend, hunger.

Halfway down the switchbacking cirque
the air is rich with double-helix
clouds of swarming mayflies,
cliff swallows taking them in flight.

## No Bite

Not enough claw
in the mountains,
not enough snow
deepening the slopes.
Not enough covert eyes,
not enough wind
to blur the vision,
not enough silence
to seize the claptrap of talk.

Not enough footprints
in the woods,
predator and prey,
no more walking sticks
left in good faith at the trailhead.
Not enough getting lost
in the back country,
exploring and holing up
on the high cliffs, the day
so long even the rocks are shaking.
Not enough bite in the winter air.

Not enough story
left in the ink,
not enough character
driven to the brink
of decision.
Not enough risk
in the telling or the living.
Not enough blood
in the word.

## Moving On

A young man follows her
from room to room, follows her
to the garden
where she goes to be alone.
Before speaking
he puts his hands on her waist.
Looking into his eyes
she thinks *so faraway and alone*
and she runs away
her fingertips on fire with not-touching.
You are beautiful, he says

to the empty space.
In the den of dark leather and fire
where the gentlemen smoke
she leans against the doorjamb,
the gnarled syllables
of politics and money
transformed by her inner ear
into animal sounds on a distant shore,
that noisy gathering together
before dispersion
into air and earth and water.

In the kitchen
her hands become birds
dropping on the rims of plates and glasses,
her face a bright pouring out of light
nodding to the talk of children and church.
She dries her hands,
staring out the window
past the trimmed hedges

to mountains rising like monuments
to the great guardians, the gods.
But even they are moving on, slowly,
like waves of land, she thinks.
Even they are leaving.

*Epilogue*

## Backing Out

Back out of this now—
Back out by retreating to the door,
  no stalling, no second guessing—
  just pulling that space together
  till it is nothing
Back out of this
  because to stay
  is to gnaw at your own spine
  from the dark niche of the stomach
  because to stay
  is to trap one voice with another
  in a small room with no windows
  only the knock on walls
  from other rooms
Back out of this—Now—
  by nodding your head
  like an old tin cup on a stick in the wind
  because the colors have all come clear
  because they are not the green you dreamed of
  but a dark shade of blue
  because the message taped on the bathroom door
  is not for you
Back out of this
  by letting the eyes go
  not your own eyes
  but hers—let them go
  to the other eyes
  let them follow
  that other path of light

## Biographical Note

Jim Peterson was born in Augusta, Georgia, raised in North Augusta, South Carolina from the age of one, and has lived in Montana and Virginia. When not writing or teaching, he enjoys riding his motorcycle around the country and hiking in the mountains and deserts of the West. His fourth poetry collection, *The Owning Stone*, won The Benjamin Saltman Award and was published in 2000 by Red Hen Press. His poetry has been widely published in such journals as *Poetry*, *Georgia Review*, *Shenandoah*, and *Prairie Schooner*, and was awarded a 2002-2003 Poetry Fellowship by the Virginia Arts Commission. His first novel, *Paper Crown*, was published in 2005 by Red Hen. He is currently Coordinator of Creative Writing at Randolph-Macon Woman's College and lives in Lynchburg, Virginia with his wife, Harriet, and their Welsh Corgi, Dylan Thomas.